FINDING QUERENCIA

MACHETE
Joy Castro, Series Editor

FINDING QUERENCIA

ESSAYS FROM IN-BETWEEN

Harrison Candelaria Fletcher

MAD CREEK BOOKS, AN IMPRINT OF
THE OHIO STATE UNIVERSITY PRESS
COLUMBUS

Library of Congress Cataloging-in-Publication Data
Names: Fletcher, Harrison Candelaria, 1962– author.
Title: Finding querencia : essays from in-between / Harrison Candelaria Fletcher.
Other titles: Machete.
Description: Columbus : Mad Creek Books, an imprint of The Ohio State University
Press, [2022] | Series: Machete | Summary: "Lyric nonfiction about building a
home from the in-between of cultures and geographies. A search for identity and
belonging within the fault-lines of New Mexican ethnicity, culture, family, and
spirit"—Provided by publisher.
Identifiers: LCCN 2021037399 | ISBN 9780814258170 (paperback) | ISBN 0814258174
(paperback) | ISBN 9780814281857 (ebook) | ISBN 9780814281857 (ebook)
Subjects: LCSH: Fletcher, Harrison Candelaria, 1962– | Racially mixed people—
Ethnic identity—Biography. | Mexican Americans—New Mexico—Biography.
| Authors, American—21st century—Biography. | BISAC: BIOGRAPHY &
AUTOBIOGRAPHY / Personal Memoirs | LITERARY COLLECTIONS /
Essays
Classification: LCC PS3606.L4767 F56 2022 | DDC 818/.609 [B]—dc23/eng/20211101
LC record available at https://lccn.loc.gov/2021037399

Cover design by Nathan Putens
Text design by Juliet Williams
Type set in Adobe Caslon Pro

For my family

Contents

Acknowledgments / ix

Prologue / xi

I **WHITE OUT** / 1

Open Season / 3

Through Walls / 8

Masked / 11

Conjugation / 14

White Out / 19

II **ORIGIN STORY** / 25

III **COYOTE LAND** / 45

Coyote Cookbook / 47

Coyote Drive-In / 51

Coyote Yearbook / 57

Of Ink Wash and Light / 61

Identity Theft / 63

Coyote Combat / 66

Coyote Curfew / 68

Imprint / 71

IV ALTAR OF LEAVES / 75

The Crossing / 77

Slightest Edge / 84

Water for Roots / 89

A Place She Goes / 94

Altar of Leaves / 97

V CONFLUENCE / 103

VI EXCAVATION / 123

VII INHERITANCE / 139

VIII BORDERLAND / 149

IX COYOTE / 159

Epilogue / 163

Acknowledgments

Some sections in this book were previously published (in different forms and sometimes with different titles) in the following journals and anthologies. Many thanks to the judges, editors, and staff who supported my work.

"Open Season," *Brevity* (selected for *The Best of Brevity: Twenty Groundbreaking Years of Flash Nonfiction* and *Advanced Creative Nonfiction: A Writer's Guide and Anthology*)

"Duke City Drive-In," *JuxtaProse* (winner of the 2019 *JuxtaProse* Nonfiction Prize published under the title "Silver Dollar Drive-In")

"Slightest Edge" and "Crossing," *Passages North* ("Crossing" nominated for Pushcart Prize)

"Identity Theft," *JuxtaProse* (finalist for *The Best of the Net* anthology)

"Identity Theft (Side B)," *Brevity* (Notable Essay, *Best American Essays 2020*)

"White Out," *Sonora Review*

"Stain," "Imprint," and "Communion," *Blue Mesa Review*

"Altar of Leaves," *Bellingham Review*

"Coyote," *Chautauqua* (published under the title, "*Origin Story: Coyote Learns to Fly*")

"Like Water for Roots," *Speculative Nonfiction*

"Coyote Cookbook," *Aquifer, The Florida Review* online (published as "Family Cookbook)

"Imprint of Passage," *Pithead Chapel*

"Coyote Combat," *Unbroken* (published as "Basic Training")

"Altar of Shadows," *Border Crossing*

"Origin Story," *Birdcoat Quarterly*

"Cutting," *Linea*

"Confluence," *Barzakh Magazine*

"Tempered," "Passages," and "Shaped," *Sierra Nevada Review*

"A Place She Goes," *Muse/A Journal* (now *Birdcoat Quarterly*)

"Conjugation," *Uproot*

Prologue

My mother, an artist and collector, spent a lifetime trying to rescue her New Mexican past. She kept her most cherished artifacts in a nickel-plated hope chest beneath our front window. Near the bottom, beneath a double-sided dowry mirror and a crown of thorns from the Penitente Brotherhood, she placed an Easter mask from the Yaqui tribe of Southern Arizona. Part-human, part-deer with a cottonwood face fringed with horsehair, the relic was as strange and beautiful as the 400-year-old ceremony from which it came— an enactment of the Passion Play with native deities and Biblical figures performing rituals from both traditions. Near the end of a weeks-long series of pageantry and dance, the masks were burned in a plaza bonfire to celebrate the resurrection of Christ.

I wasn't supposed to play with it, which meant, of course, I did. Once summer evening while my mother tended her roses de Castilla outside, I slipped on the rough-hewn face covering and stood before our broad living room mirror. I remember being terrified by the cobwebs brushing my cheeks and the suffocating smell of mothballs and mold. But it was the eyes that held me—my eyes—shining like opals beneath the twisted animal features and bringing the spirit to life as if some hidden side of me had stepped out from the trove of memory. Standing before my reflection, it wasn't the pascola face that scared me, but what I recognized behind it. Wearing the mask, I saw myself.

I

WHITE OUT

Open Season

Here they come coyote with their switchblade smiles wearing adobe and denim to twist back time in your junior high halls with bounties on blondes, blue eyes and braces to reseed alfalfa on subdivision lawns to carve Spanish accents on white picket fences to raise Chicano fists high as hawks to dance with history on the New Mexican fault line out for fun out for blood out for you.

*

- to combine from different ingredients
- to form a whole whose constituent parts are distinct
- to juxtapose
- to join unlike elements: i.e., oil and water.

*

Here they come coyote, the Speedy Gonzales cartoons, the Frito Bandito erasers, the Ricky Ricardo's "Got some splainin' to do," the Ricardo Mantalbán's "Corinthian leather," *The Treasure of Sierra Madre* "no stinking badges," the Taco Bell chihuahua and "run for the border," the Telly Savalas as Pancho Villa, the Marlon Brando as Emiliano Zapata, the Looney Tunes wolf in Zoot Suit clothing, the low-rider steering wheel made from chrome chains.

*

"I don't feel comfortable calling myself that."
   "But it's who you are."
   "It doesn't feel right."
   "Why not?"
   "Look at me."

*

Here they come coyote with their tortilla sandwiches with their hand-me-down eyes with their South Valley soil still staining their shoes with their English textbooks wrapped in brown paper bags all the boys you and your white friends point to and smile.

*

IS THIS PERSON OF HISPANIC, LATINX, OR SPANISH ORIGIN?

☐ Yes, Mexican, Mexican Am., Chicano
☐ Yes, Puerto Rican
☐ Yes, Cuban
☐ No, not of Hispanic, Latinx, or Spanish Origin
☐ No

*

Here they come coyote the Friday night sleepovers at the neighbor's house the shag carpet dens the double-quilted couches the color TVs the milk and cookies the Pat Nixon pearls the Archie Bunker recliners the silent wish they would ask you to stay.

*

1. *The advantages and/or immunities certain groups benefit from based on appearance*
2. *Not having to worry about being followed in a department store while shopping*
3. *Seeing your image on television*
4. *Having others assume you lead a constructive life free of crime; of Welfare.*
5. *Having the luxury to fight racism one day and ignore it the next.*
6. *Never having to think about it.*

*

Here they come coyote the deceased older father you never really knew the deceased father's family you never really knew the Scottish-French ghosts who left your name and your skin and your slot machine genes through your fingers like change.

*

a. *a Spanish corruption of a Nahuatl word*
b. *of half-Spanish and half-Anglo decent*
c. *rebels against social convention with deception/ humor*

d. [slang] a contemptible person, avaricious or dis-
*   honest*
e. both hunter and scavenger [i.e., opportunist]
f. trickster, transformer, shape-shifter
g. thief

*

Here they come coyote the eight shades of brown of your mother's siblings skin and the highway crew calluses on your grandfather's hands and the farmland furrows on your grandmother's face and the single-mom defiance in your single mom's stare and the beans and green chile feeding your soul and the flour tortillas you fold like a spoon and the ten-speed bike you make from stolen parts and the tangled roots from New Mexico to Spain and the box you leave blank on government forms and the R's you roll from your tongue like dice.

*

"Welcome to the Diversity Committee. Thank you all for coming. Why don't we start by introducing ourselves. How about you? Down there in the back. Tell us: Why are *you* here?"

*

Here they come coyote the Mexican mirrors you will hang from your walls. The red-brown soil you will keep in a jar. The hand-carved santos watching over your home. The Latina you will marry in a 200-year-old adobe church. The Spanish family names you will give to your children. The red chile enchiladas you will make to perfection. The ranchera songs you will play each Christmas. The Southwestern skies you will swim in your sleep. Your mother's maiden name you will add to your own. Your mother's own words that will sting like a slap, "Funny you would do that, I always thought you were more Anglo."

*

Here they come coyote they caught your scent at last with your head down low at your bottom-tier locker with the combination spinning between your two best friends between the blond one and brown one between lie and another better run better hide better choose.

Through Walls

1.

/ Born of a man / who wore a white smock / behind a white counter / with mortar, pestle / scales and tubes / mixing chemical elements / to heal the afflicted / and later in life / alone in his garage / with pollen, seeds / soil and stems / grafting hybrids / bound at their wounds. /

2.

/ Born of a woman / who drove into the desert / seeking the rust and bone / of what might have been / or never actually was / driftwood and wire / nailed to her walls / with peeling mirrors / and shrines of stone / outside her window / a meadowlark pierces / a veil of wind. /

3.

/ Born of a land / on the vanishing point / of a green bowl valley / a broad blue mountain / a shallow brown river / coming up fast / in your rearview mirror / with interstate stripes / you never connect. /

4.

/ Born of a past / grown heavy in your pockets / high desert stones / gathered like eggs / your mother beside you / warming the shells / to blossom with feathers / bright flames in her eyes / a double vision / you, too, can see / both of you peeling / a rind from the sky. /

5.

/ Born of a prayer / the one prayer you know / olive-wood beads / tight to your chest / rubbed smooth / rubbed raw / over-working the words / all you don't know / all you can't say / if you only you knew / how to feel belief / the weight of your silence / would slip from its chain. /

6.

/ Born of a state / a transitional process / straddling posi-
tions / on both sides of a line / a singular obsession / endlessly
revised / ambivalent / contradictory / conflicting / confused / a
stage of suffering / of expiating sin / half / here / half / there /
across / into / at / between. /

7.

/ Born of an absence / just over your shoulder / or under your
bed / around a corner / misplacing keys / forgetting your wal-
let / holding the smoke / where your father once stood / your
mother once stood / you yourself once stood / where one
shape ends / another begins. /

8.

/ Born of a dream / of walking through walls / with shape-
shifting skin / X-ray eyes / a comic book hero / with one-
thousand faces / a time-traveling trickster / exorcising demons
/ out-running ghosts / his secret power / embracing the dis-
tinction / of no distinctions at all. /

Masked

1.

Coyote lights a fire
With brown paper
Scraps
At the school bus stop
Where his misfit friends scale
Cinderblock walls
To stand beside him
Swallowing flame with their
Eyes.

2.

Coyote parts his hair
Straight down the middle
To tame a part of himself
Refusing to lie flat
Or do what it's told

Like irrigation water from
His family's acequia
Always jumping the berms
Always flooding the gutters
Always puddling the street
Causing neighbors to yell
When will you learn to
Stay in your place.

3.

Coyote draws an eagle
On the back of a quarter
For his art class portrait
Always coming up tails
When called in the air
By critics who wonder
How he learned to draw
As though precise imitation
Could break his fall.

4.

Coyote wears a mask
From monsters he made with
Matches and rubber with
Razor blade grafts with

New heads on necks
New arms on shoulders
New feet on legs he melts
Himself into a way to
Behave.

5.

Coyote makes a skin
From bones in his throat
Shining white at night
From house to house with his
Brown sack open as candy
Rains down with cellophane smiles
At his costume of choice
With his insides out
He looks so real.

Conjugation

1.

INGLÉS: "*Who are you?*"
ESPAÑOL: "*¿Quién eres?*"

Your teenage daughter has begun teaching herself Spanish, as the new kid in another new school. If she can say the words right, she says to you, maybe she can finally fit in.

2.

INGLÉS: "*What are you?*"
ESPAÑOL: "*¿Qué eres?*"

It is you, she reminds you, who moved your family cross-country to be closer to their roots, but the roots she knows, are as tangled as yours, buried in decades of doubt.

3.

INGLÉS: "*What are we?*"

ESPAÑOL: "*¿Qué somos?*"

Noun: coy·ote /ˈkī͵ōt, kīˈōdē/ [*canis latrans*] swift carnivorous mammal; hunts singly or in small groups; known for its various distinctive vocalizations (cry, howl, song).

4.

INGLÉS: "*Who am I?*"

ESPAÑOL: "*¿Quién soy?*"

If she speaks Spanish, she tries to explain, she won't feel so much like a fraud. But you are who you are, you respond sincerely. Yet, you both know who you're trying to convince.

5.

INGLÉS: "*Who are you?*"

ESPAÑOL: "*¿Quién eres tú?*"

You joined a gang in junior high, if you could call it that, since Los Zorros lasted a month. The outlaw image suited your Hispanic friends, but for you, it was always the mask.

6.

INGLÉS: "*Who are we?*"

ESPAÑOL: "*¿Quiénes somos?*"

Your daughter met a boy with Mexican parents, who raised him to speak only English. When they whisper in Spanish, behind his back, they think he can't understand, but he does.

7.

INGLÉS: "*What are we?*

ESPAÑOL: "*¿Qué somos?*"

You asked your mother why she never taught you Spanish, and she said you never wanted to know, which wasn't right, the never wanting, you just didn't know what you wanted to know.

8.

INGLÉS: "*We are . . .*"

ESPAÑOL: "*Somos. . . .*"

Your daughter met a girl, born in Guatemala, who helps pound her tin accent into silver. This courage your daughter has, you wished you possessed, tempering one voice from two.

9.

INGLÉS: "*You are . . .*"

ESPAÑOL: "*Usted es . . .*"

"So, what are you then?" asks the woman at the diversity mixer, but when you respond with a question, she says with a shrug, "If you don't know, then maybe you're nothing."

10.

INGLÉS: "*I am . . .*"

ESPAÑOL: "*Yo soy . . .*"

Your daughter is joining a Latinx club at school, but fears they might laugh when she speaks, so she changes her smartphone to all-Spanish text, and whispers to the screen in the dark.

11.

INGLÉS: "*What are you?*"

ESPAÑOL: "*¿Qué eres?*"

Print here _____

12.

INGLÉS: "*We are . . .*"

ESPAÑOL: "*Somos . . .*"

Your daughter texts you an emoji, without translation, before her first Latinx Club meeting: a dark gray disc, with silvery edges—a mask, a mirror, a moon.

White Out

1. Note from HR—

Dear Employee:

According to our records, you have listed two different names in your personnel file:

- *A first and last name*
- *A first, last,* and *middle name that does not correspond with your original application documents*

We are in the process of verifying your correct identifying information with the State of Colorado. Please advise.

2. Name /nām/ noun—

- A word or set of words by which a person, animal, place, or thing is known.
- A word or symbol used to designate an entity
- Appearance as opposed to reality

3. Phone Call—

Your mother has something to tell you. Yes, she's fine. It's nothing like that. Listen: Did you know the name she's used her entire life—her first name—isn't her real name? No. Never was. Well, when her family left New Mexico for Southern California during World War II (so your grandfather could work in the shipyards), she enrolled in elementary school, and her teacher couldn't pronounce her first name, which means queen in Spanish, so she wrote another name—an Anglo name—on her transcripts instead. From that day on she was referred to at school by that Anglo name. And it stuck. Never mind that no one in her family ever used it, the Anglo name remained on her permanent record and official documents. Isn't that terrible? How someone can take your name and erase your identity as though you never existed? She's been thinking about that lately. She thought you'd want to know.

4. Question from Your Daughter—

Dad, can I ask you something? You know how we always have these long conversations about ethnic identity? And how it bothers me when people ask me what I am, and when I tell them, they don't always believe me? And how you're always telling me I'm Latina no matter what anyone else says, because Mom is full and you're half? Well, I've been thinking. I'd like to change my last name. Instead of your name, I'd like to use Mom's maiden name, a Spanish name, instead. To reflect who I really am. What do you think?

5. Origin Story—

- Your father was the last in his family line.
- When he died of lung cancer in August 1964, he left no relatives, no friends, few heirlooms, no history.
- But he did have one thing:
- His name.
- Which he left to you.
- To keep alive.

6. Fletcher—

/ˈfleCHər/ Middle English: occupational. Taken from the primary vocation of an ancestor; one who makes arrows, (flech(i)er/ fleche 'arrow'); *verb*—"to fletch," "to furnish (an arrow) with a feather." Arrow: symbol of swiftness, movement, purpose, decision.

7. Phone Call—

Your mother has something else to tell you: Remember what she said about her first name? Well, she decided to change it. Yes. She's taking back her original name. But that's not what she wanted to tell you. Listen: Did you know that for the majority of her life she's gone by her married name? And that all official documents refer to her as "Mrs." Well, that may have been true at one point in her life, but she's not that person anymore. So, she's decided to return to her maiden name. She's changing her first *and* last name. Because she's 83 years old and wants to die as the person she is and not the person others made her through labels and naming. What do you think?

8. Candelaria—

[kan-deh-laA-ria] Gender Feminine. Origin: Spanish; *Candle-mas,* derived from *candela,* candle. In honor of the church festival of Candlemas, which commemorates the presentation of Christ in the temple and the purification of the Virgin Mary. Associated with the appearance of a Virgin Mary statue on the island of Tenerife in 1392. The statue held a child in one arm and a green candle in her other hand (hence "Candelaria"). It was discovered on the beach of Chimisay by two goatherders. One man tried to throw a stone at the statue but his arm became paralyzed. The other tried to stab the statue with a knife but ended up stabbing himself. Considered miraculous. The statue was enshrined as "Nuestra Senora de la Candelaria" (Our Lady of the Light).

9. HR Form—

Please select the box that best describes the race/ethnicity category with which you primarily identify. Select ONLY one.

10. Advice from a Friend—

Ok. Let me see if I get it: After your father died, you were raised entirely by your mother's family with the Latinx culture and traditions of New Mexico. And now, as you reconnect to those roots, you want to add your mother's maiden name to your own legal name to reflect who you are and where you come from. But you don't speak much Spanish, you don't look Latinx, and none of your five siblings use your mother's maiden name. And because of that, you're concerned about the appearance of cultural appropriation, capitalizing on a minority status, and being seen as a "Born Again Hispanic?" My advice: You worry too much. It's only a name, right?

11. Name/*transitive verb*—
   1. to label
   2. to assign meaning
   3. to accuse
   4. to nominate
   5. to define
   6. to legitimize
   7. to choose

12. Response to Your Daughter—
Yes, I understand why you want to drop your last name—my last name—and use your mom's maiden name instead. And yes, regardless of what anyone says, you are—by blood—three-quarters Latinx, even if you have the same light coloring as me. But now, I have a question for you: Wouldn't erasing your last name also be an inaccurate representation of who you are? You're a person of mixed ethnicity, right? Would not keeping your last name represent that truth as well?

13. Response from Your Daughter—
Can we not talk about this anymore?

14. Phone Call—
Your mother has yet another thing to tell you. Yes, she did indeed change her name—both names. But that's not what she wants to tell you. Listen: While she was sitting in the

Vital Records Department haggling with bureaucrats about forms and documents and which boxes to check, she got to talking with all the old Spanish people around her. And you know what? They were changing their names, too. They had all been given new names in school when they were little—Anglo names—and now they wanted to take them back. Yes. It's true. A whole room full of people her same age taking back their true identities once and for all. Isn't that something?

15. WO-1 Erasing Liquid—

"Covers even the toughest mistakes . . ."

16. Check Mark—

☐ A person who primarily identifies with two or more ethnicity categories.

17. Clarification from Your Daughter—

Dad, you *do* realize that even having this discussion—even having the ability to choose which box to check—is itself an example of white privilege, right? And that we continue to benefit from it? Ok. Just making sure.

18. Note from IT Department—

Dear User:

It has come to our attention that the name on your email application does not match the name in your personnel file. In the interests of security, please contact us at your earliest convenience. This may represent an attempt at identity theft.

II

ORIGIN STORY

1.

A colleague listens to you read about your childhood among
cottonwoods, owls, acequias, arroyos, and the apple-skin New
Mexican sky. Afterward, he places a hand on your shoulder.
You are, he says, the most haunted person he knows.

2.

You sit as a boy on the hardwood floor of your home, beside rocks from the river, deer antlers from the llano, and a castle of Cochiti drums. With knights and monsters, you drift through wood-smoke incense and the watery light from the front window. You are flying, or swimming, in a story or a dream, trying hard to never touch down.

3.

Your grandmother watches you across the kitchen table while your mother makes fried potatoes and tortillas for supper. You move like your father, she says to you smiling, but since you don't remember him, you have nothing to say, and return instead to your toys. She tries again, in Spanish, but you still don't respond, so she frowns at your mother. He's like Pinocchio, your grandmother says. Boy of wood: Half self, half soul.

4.

Growing up, you are often asked a question about yourself and our family origins you can't easily answer. Your silence is filled by others. Almost always to your benefit.

5.

During lunch in junior high, Chicano boys gather outside the cafeteria to throw milk cartons across the quad at Anglo students. Pints explode white against hair, clothes, books, and skin. The stain remains throughout the day. Sometimes you throw a carton. Sometimes the target is you.

6.

As an adult, you visit your brother-in-law in Albuquerque
after having left for a job in Denver. Your brother-in-law, like
your wife, has deep New Mexican roots. Over enchiladas he
asks how you're adjusting. You tell him Colorado is like a nice
apartment, but will never be home. It's too white. He pauses,
fork suspended. What do you mean? he asks, *You're* white.

7.

At a cafeteria in a Northeastern college you sit across the table from a Black colleague during breakfast. You get to talking about where you're from and where you live, and he asks what you thought of Richmond, Virginia, where you lived four years before returning to Colorado. You tell him Richmond was lush, beautiful, and rich with history, but as a New Mexican, you felt out of place, particularly when passing the monuments to Confederate generals. That's not your history, you tell him. He frowns. But it is, he says. It *is* your history. You try to clarify. Your Southwestern legacy is equally oppressive and bloody—genocide of Native peoples by Spanish conquistadors, then Manifest Destiny—but not the Confederacy, not that. He begins to speak, decides something, finishes his breakfast. Gazing into your cup, you see your mask, and turn away.

8.

You paint the same image again and again of your maternal grandfather, maternal grandmother, infant mother, and two of her nine siblings squinting under the sun of a river valley field. From your basement walls you trace their eyes beyond the frame, imagining you feel what they see.

9.

Your mother phones to tell you she dreamed about you again wading through a river, veering from one bank to another, seeking something you'd lost. She tried to tell you to stay where you were, but you couldn't hear, as though you were partitioned behind glass. She knows you don't believe her, she says, hanging up, but she had to tell you anyway. But you believe, you say. You believe.

10.

A friend from Southern California visits your home and surveys your displays of New Mexican santos, retablos, crucifixes, and ceremonial Native American artwork, and says he had no idea you were so religious. You don't know how to respond. You dropped out of Catechism in the second grade. You never attend church. You don't even know how to pray.

11.

You collect since childhood desert rocks, roots, and leaves, and assemble them into tabletop shrines. But the more you gather, the more you realize how many have begun to resemble graves.

12.

A college friend of your wife's visits Colorado after driving up from New Mexico, where he remained after graduation. It has been a while since they have seen each other, and they begin reminiscing about their university days in Las Cruces, and where their group eventually settled. After a pause, he sets down his beer and folds his arms. Strange, he says, how many of his friends still identify as New Mexican despite having left decades earlier pursuing careers, relationships, or other opportunities. He himself decided to stay, but he doesn't begrudge anyone for their choices. Yet, he remains bewildered at their emotional investment in being considered New Mexicans when they return to visit. But they're not, he says, turning to you. They're tourists.

13.

Your friends and family don't understand why you write the way you do: in fragments and run-ons with gaps and white spaces and multiple shape-shifting perspectives. Why, they ask, don't you just come out and say what you mean? But you are, you reply. That's what you mean.

14.

You remember taking a phone call from a Hispanic man who read your column in Albuquerque's afternoon paper about preserving Southwestern culture, roots, and tradition, but your story didn't match your byline or photo, so he wondered aloud if you were a thief. Why, he asked, were you pretending to be something you were not? Why, he wondered, were you adopting a heritage from others? When you tried to explain, he gave you a name, New Mexican slang for mixed race, mixed ethnicity, mongrel. Coyote, he said. That's what you are. Coyote is exactly what you are.

15.

[coyote | *'kī̲ ōt, kī'ōdē* |]: Middleman, smuggler, counterfeiter, thief. Crossing borders without impediment. Runs from one town to another but belongs to neither. Marked by hybridity constantly negotiated. Cobbles reality from a bricolage of materials. Took smooth rivers and made them twist and turn. Restores balance by reconfiguring pain. Absorbs grief otherwise lodged in shadow. Ran and got a poker and began raking ashes. Didn't run straight but zig-zagged all around. Looked for the one he had thrown away. Held a stone in his palm. Closed his eyes. Began to sing.

16.

Questions from reader: What is the role of identity in this essay? Is this essay detailing a lost identity, or an identity the narrator was born into, but not necessarily representative of? Is it an identity based on a distant heritage, or an identity estranged from close heritage? Each time she reads it, she comes to a different conclusion. Can you explain? What is this essay meant to explore?

17.

Response to a reader: You never swam as a boy in the suburban-heights pools, with their blue-eyed water, and white-tiled teeth, and chlorine stinging like shame. You preferred instead the shallow mountain streams and the earthen acequias of the Rio Grande farmland. But you really couldn't swim, so you stayed close to the edges, where your toes could always touch down. And yet, there were moments, when you waded into the current, threw back your head, and drifted.

III

COYOTE LAND

Coyote Cookbook

BEANS

Because they're cheap and they're good and they always last longer than the government checks boiling slowly away in the Pyrex pot on the open blue flame building pressurized steam to slow-cook the garlic and bay leaves and olive oil to a river-brown broth soaking down your roots to bloom from your bones to fill up your table at supper.

TORTILLAS

Which you love more than bread but never get right with an ingredient missing from the salt shortening and flour that sticks to your skin with a white you can't wash so you form instead an imperfect ball rolled into the shape of a ghost ship from Iowa where your father came from before he sighed through the curtains of his hospital room to fill your house with a silent moon on a cast-iron comal while you wait with a plate the size of the hole in your stomach.

ENCHILADAS

Rolled up tight or laid out and layered like your mother's whole family in the back of the Buick on a bed of quilts as warm as onions and cheese while they drive from Corrales to Los Angeles again so your grandfather can paint enough wartime destroyers to fill the nine mouths fast asleep through the desert with road stripes stabbing like forks and knives to pull them apart before they're ready.

HAMBURGER MEAT AND FRIED POTATOES

Filling the whole pan like the family reunion in your grandparent's backyard for the cottonwood snapshot of Uncle Mike and his Schlitz and Tony's Dean Martin sheen and Georgina's Rita Moreno smile and Uncle Sam's pointing finger and your mom's La Raza eyes and everyone mingling like salt and pepper made moist from the steam to stick together only to come undone like a mismatched salad of crispy and soft that still feeds you like nothing else can.

CHILINDRON

Because you never eat turkey on Thanksgiving Day since your mother adopted stray ducks geese and owls and planted a branch of dried cedar in a tub of rocks from the river where your Christmas tree stood and said "being different is good" and if you really want to know she's more Basque than Latina and made of garlic and red peppers and ham and chicken and lemon and white wine and Spanish olives and Roma tomatoes still retaining their flavor while simmering whole and isn't that the whole point of sustenance anyway.

SMOTHERED STEAK

Your deceased father's favorite pounded soft with a mallet until the muscle breaks down and the fiber gives way and the Gold Medal flour is forced deep into the folds and served up with thick gravy and drowned Southern-style like a history you don't know and a family you can't name and a serving you can't swallow no matter how hard you chew.

OATMEAL

Because your dogs will eat anything when that's all there is.

POSOLE

Steaming the kitchen windows red amber and green through the Christmas Eve boil of pork hominy garlic you see your own face staring in from outside like a ghost on the ditch bank on the way home from school with a hand raised hello like the dreams of your father who was born on this day and now waits all alone with photos in the closet to swallow the moths of the memories that pass like snow drifting down into brown paper bag candles filling with feathers of light.

CHILE

Green as the cottonwoods outside your window the water in the acequia behind your house and the sky in the morning when you walk to school with a taste in your mouth that won't go away like the roasting drums on the North Valley road where the capsaicin smoke as bright as the emulsion on the back of your eyes with images etched deep this permanent reminder the burn you feel is real.

CINNAMON BREAD

Because it wasn't as bad as it might seem and sometimes you woke from your afternoon nap to find your mother in an apron at the kitchen counter with white dusted flour and brown sparkle sugar making from scratch a kneaded loaf with a yin-yang eye spiraling toward a center uniquely its own to show what she said and what you try to believe that yes being mixed can be good.

Coyote Drive-In

THE GREAT RACE

We started out strong on the first of each month shopping
carts poised as if Kmart were Paris when the gun finally
sounded we dashed through the aisles gathering milk, fruit,
potatoes and sacks of beans just one step ahead of the black
cape of fate through Arabian sand and Carpanian Alps as glo-
rious as a pie fight we picked out boxes of Betty Crocker one
flavor per kid to keep our eyes on the distant glow of *Lost in
Space* and *All in the Family* while the refrigerator bulb burned
bright on fumes we pushed ahead through the cashier line
knowing our hunger would carry us through.

A MAN CALLED HORSE

Always the Indians never the cowboys through the front yard
sunflowers throwing Russian olive spears at cardboard Cav-
alry riding over the hills from subdivision rooftops as white
as the screen where we imaged ourselves tied down held cap-
tive by shimmering frames of Manifest Destiny tossing scraps
and kicking us outside to sleep with the dogs with ethnici-
ties uncertain we had to prove ourselves during midnight raids
to assassinate doubts of which side we were on so we grew
out our hair and burned cedar incense and rose toward the
light with eagle claws piercing the muscles in our chests with
tie-dye flaming through the ash of convention we found our
tribe yet stood apart like an Englishman warrior among Hol-
lywood Sioux and still we came back to watch it again memo-
rizing the words until we were certain which script told the lie.

PLANET OF THE APES

We lived in a house where animals ruled or a least roamed
free after landing off course on their way to the river or
sometimes appearing in cardboard boxes left at our door
by people who knew we took in strays after our father died
our mother had wanted us to learn how to heal by nurturing the wounded until our backyard seemed like a whole other
world grown wild with lilacs and roses and stones where the
only cages were turned inside out by a single woman and
her five young children wide-eyed with survival and something like grief unable to speak to the ghost on the porch
with the pharmacist's smock and Pall Malls gone cold while
the peacock and owl and snow geese and mallards gave voice
to the language of grace and feathers revealed to neighbors who scowled through their curtains at the science-fic-
tion scene unfolding before them to drop to their knees at
the realization the Statue of Liberty was there all along.

BEN HUR

Our horseshoe driveway became a chariot race through dirt
and gravel on rampaging bikes while our mother sat watching from the front porch steps her hand held poised for the
thumbs up or thumbs down for the biblical tale of rags to
riches chasing the neighbors in endless circles forever com-
paring their haves to our nots their sissy bar chrome and star-
burst paint against our rust bolt wire and spray paint tape and
just when we caught them their W. A. S. P. stingers flashed
like blades from their wheels to chew up our spokes and send
us sprawling yet still we believed in whispering to horses
its own kind of faith like rain washing down cleansing lep-
rosy wounds or offering a drink to a man carrying a cross his
thirst was our strength as nobility's son was dragged through
dirt when trumpets finally sounded we held our own reins.

THE GOOD, THE BAD, AND THE UGLY

Growing up on our block it sometimes seemed like our mother stood alone in a three-way gunfight on the Vietnam War with one neighbor's "America: Love It or Leave It" and another neighbor's "Nattering nabobs of negativism" while she held her ground with her finger on the trigger of a "Nixon No" sign with a swastika "X" while they all kept their eyes on the eyes of the others in the high desert sun from face to face the tension taut as a guitar string soundtrack our mother shot holes in their "Firing Line" lines with her dead-eye wit she walked grave to grave past the unmarked headstone meant for her brother as the draft blew by leaving us chilled to the bone.

IT'S A MAD MAD MAD MAD WORLD

On weekends we scrambled into a metallic green Comet or a
powder blue Ford for a madcap dash toward whispered treasure beneath three crossed palms on a horizon bright as our
grandmother's dream of gold coins buried within camposanto
bones our fingers reaching through hot sand and grass for
all we lost and hoped to retrieve each thorn and leaf a self-
portrait shrine we nailed with keys to our mother's white walls
pointing the way to the living room hope chest beneath the
front window to the spot marked "X" creaking open the hinges
to a blossom of dust rising into the light.

Coyote Yearbook

1. Cafeteria tables arms folded in shadow.
2. Sunlight spilling milk through the door.
3. Bleach, boiled carrots, and possibly cake.
4. Two shuffling lines a stool on a stage.
5. Spotlights, backdrop, a stool on a stage.
6. The white picket fence of the cameraman's smile.
7. The G.I. Joe crewcut of the cameraman's smile.
8. The G.I. Joe scar of the cameraman's smile.
9. Bag of shiny black combs like a bucket of snakes.
10. Bucket of snakes like barrels of guns.
11. Barrels of guns like the cameraman's eyes.
12. Cameraman's eyes on your McGovern lapel pin.
13. McGovern lapel pin and your John Lennon hair.
14. Your John Lennon hair and the comb in your hand.
15. Comb in your hand like the butt of a joke.
16. Butt of a joke like the cameraman's smile.
17. The hush of your classmates at his finger in your chest.
18. The anger of his words as hot as his lamps.
19. *With hair like that you should stand with the girls.*
20. Laughter leaking through hand-covered mouths.

21. Spaces around you as your friends step away.

22. Shiny black barrels of combs in their hands

23. Combs in their hands aimed straight at your chest.

24. Firing squad chants of *Bang! You're dead!*

25. The stars and stripes of the cameraman's smile.

26. The trickle of light your eyes follow out the door.

27. The door you open while standing in place.

28. Standing in place thumbing teeth on the comb.

29. Teeth of the comb like calliope notes.

30. Calliope notes like chimes on your porch.

31. Chimes on your porch like the vines of campana de oro.

32. Campana de oro like sparrows and doves.

33. Sparrows and doves like a Jemez Mountain stream.

34. Jemez Mountain stream like rosaries on your walls.

35. Rosaries on your walls like your paper route quarters.

36. Paper route quarters like stacked monthly bills.

37. Stacked monthly bills like your mother cleaning beans.

38. Your mother cleaning beans like her pet owl watching sparrows.

39. Pet owl watching sparrows like the sun through her turquoise windows.

40. The sun through her turquoise windows like the patrolman's flashing lights.

41. The patrolman's flashing lights outside a high plains cowboy town.

42. Outside a high plains cowboy town pulled over for *Looking suspicious.*

43. Pulled over for *Looking suspicious* in long hair and tie-dye shirts.

44. In long hair and tie-dyed shirts on a Sunday drive exploring the desert.

45. On a Sunday drive exploring the desert a crewcut cop with 20 questions.

46. Crewcut cop with 20 questions mispronouncing your mother's name.

47. Mispronouncing your mother's name she asks him to define *Looking suspicious.*

48. She asks him to define *Looking suspicious* and he defines it by describing us.

49. He defines it by describing us and your mother says *Go ahead and arrest me.*

50. Your mother says *Go ahead and arrest me so you can feel like a real man.*

51. *So you can feel like a real man harassing a widow and her five young kids.*

52. A widow and her five young kids in the patrolman's mirror shades.

53. In patrolman's shades the flash of handcuffs on his hip.

54. The flash of handcuffs on his hip like the polish of resentment.

55. The polish of resentment in the eyes of you and your mother.

56. In the eyes of you and your mother he rips a ticket from his book.

57. He rips a ticket from his book summoning your mother before a judge.

58. Your mother before a judge says her only crime is being herself.

59. Her only crime is being herself fills the silence of the courtroom.

60. In the silence of the courtroom charges drop with a wooden gavel.

61. Charges drop with a wooden gavel on your mother's bravest face.

62. On your mother's bravest face she runs a hand along your hair.

63. She runs a hand along your hair as you memorize her expression.

64. You memorize her expression the cameraman says cheese.

65. The cameraman says cheese through his muzzle-flashing bulbs.

66. Through his muzzle-flashing bulbs you return your mother's smile.

Of Ink Wash and Light

At the end of September your mother and uncle open a fine arts booth at the Spanish Village of the New Mexico State Fair selling charcoal drawings, sepia washes, and glass figurines of the farmers, vaqueros and Navajo shepherds erased from the landscapes around them. You stay home from school to help monitor the displays and during lulls in traffic walk frame to frame as if watching a prayer drift across the windshield of your grandfather's pickup finding its way back home. Memories rise like dust on the dashboard and you breathe them in with a delicate sorrow filtering down to the sand in your pockets from the Jemez Mountain stream you try to cross each summer and return with cut-offs stained with a rust your mother can never wash clean.

One night you hear a drum and follow the beat to a circle of streetlight in the adobe plaza of the Indian Village where a crowd assembles around an Apache dancer whirling through wood smoke and moths. Muscled, bare-chested, streaked with ash he wears a black hood with two holes for eyes and a head-dress of crosses or horns. He swings in an arc a long leather thong with a thin wooden disc whirring loud as a hornet through leaping silver conchos and a blurred red sash. He is beautiful and terrifying a deity made flesh chasing shadows from the sand as you approach.

With the boom in your belly and cedar-burned eyes you dizzy yourself trying to follow his spirals the sensation of sinking underwater again in the Jemez Mountain stream kicking hard through a current of sepia stains pulled hard dragged down by the memory of a longing you can't quite reach to neither hold nor release behind windshield glass you forget to breathe the sand through your pockets is sifting away you break to the surface drawing air through a dream the figurine dancer with his hand reaching out.

Without even thinking you step out beside him into the space he creates on the dust-stained canvas of ink wash and light between erasure and promise you teach yourself how to swim.

Identity Theft

1—Monsters

in your palm at the T. G.& Y. toy aisle with the drunks on the
ditch bank and the bloody pet duck and the fist through the
window all snug in your pockets with rubber snakes and plastic bats and severed lizard heads kept close as your nightmares
you make them your friends.

2—Change

from the puddle of your uncle's denim jeans by his floorboard
mattress you move unseen with fingers worms crawling toward
catfish quarters for a drug store sucker with a gold star sticker
the shimmer of a promise you just might reach if you hold
your breath and glide unseen through a cross-current culture
of Anglo and Chicano and spaces between.

3—*Mad* magazine

slipped under the front of your shirt while the pharmacist pre-
tends to see only his work you sit alone later on your bedroom floor with Risk and Clue a padlocked door folding the

back pages until two edges meet into a unified shape you try
to believe.

4—Hostess apple pie

in your back jeans pocket like a sugar-coated myth like a July
Fourth rocket like the American Dream you never believed
like the cop car lecture like your silent reprieve like pulling up
your bootstraps would never explain your impulse to steal was
never about pain.

5—Heirloom

lifted from your father's closet box a black cashmere sweater
by a broken clock too short on the arms too tight on the chest
in the davenport snapshot he looks off to his left at a noise or
a blur just edging into view in his half-smiling eyes you hope
it was you.

6—Brach's penny candy

from the Foodway aisle you pass unseen with your white
father's smile as the Anglo clerk stalks your Hispanic friend
the security guard approaches from the opposite end while you
slip outside picking caramel from your teeth knowing in your
bones what makes you the thief.

7—Mask

from the hope chest against the front window a cottonwood
spirit of horsehair and sinew with ghost eyes you walk down
the junior high hall to follow a voice a persistent call an illu-

sion of rescue in your mother's tracks as if Yaqui drums could
resurrect your past.

8–Buick LaSabre

with headlights off in the backseat buzzing with screwdriver
shots the S-curve gravity holding you down the face in the
window the face of the drowned when red lights flash and
everyone flees you remain seatbelted in place by the reflection
you see.

9—Marlboros

taken from the 7-Eleven counter cannot soothe like cedar
sawdust powder sprinkled over the furnace on the living room
floor to singe your legs to bathe your soul from her aspen
perch your pet owl watches you rise to curl like an embryo
into the flame of her eyes.

Coyote Combat

Hunting shadows in the South Pacific jungle
of your North Valley yard silent as a toad under
streetlamp light your deceased father
beside you like a moth in the closet still drawn
to the photos in the bottom of a box you can never
quite reach to capture or kill or just let go
this stalking this searching this hand on your shoulder
raising the barrel at the boy in your sights.

*

Hanging in place from the backyard swings
your big brother's broomstick a drill sergeants' baton
he's making you a man don't talk don't cry don't dare
let go he's trying to teach you how to survive
he knows what he means he remembers himself
behind the enemy lines of his silence.

*

Dodging artillery dirt clods and rocks
your trashcan-lid shield a moving target
as shrapnel explodes your brother tells you
to remember to die with both hands raised
as if raking clouds or pulling down curtains
across your window still holding smoke
from snuffed Pall Malls still lingering
with mothballs in the closet.

*

Lighting a match for the man on the grill
his bayonet held high through gusts of laughter
and lighter fluid smoke this ghost left watching
from toys on the floor his featureless face
as smooth as a jungle just burn it all down
just start it all over with a pyre or a prayer
or some kind of penance plastic beads into ash.

*

Lobbing grenades from a carton of eggs
at distant headlights along Guadalupe Trail
a runway of bombers always coming or going
but never remaining to see you standing in
beer bottle butts two hands to your chest
as if cradling a bird still tending a presence
in the bottom of a box
from dust to desire to flame.

Coyote Curfew

/ Becoming scared all over again / rising into the night / to steal what we could / to burn what we could / to break what we could / with ax-handles / mallets / and toys from the yard / hitting the walls hard / to harden our knuckles / alive with the stars / and the firewood smoke / as smooth as shadows / through the streetlamp light / bathed in silver / as if we were clean. /

*

/ Becoming scared all over again / inhaling embers / prescription pill powder / a neighbor's mirror / his mother a nurse / looking up symptoms / in medical books / may cause drowsiness dizziness slurring / do not take with alcohol / hold tight / both hands on the rails / the centrifugal force / timing the release / at just the right time / to mark off with chalk / the contours of our fall. /

*

/ Becoming scared all over again / your brother on his knees /
the couch a pew / his head on a pillow / our mother's lap / she
scratches his back / she smooths his hair / his eyes like shot
glasses / burn with fuel / outrunning static / from the hallway
closet / our father's short-wave radio / tuned to a frequency /
your brother still hears / in spaces / dashes / etched in scars /
on both of his fists. /

*

/ Becoming scared all over again / on your stomach on the
ditch bank / a handful of rocks / a head full of smoke / the
midnight traffic on Guadalupe Trail / a pilgrimage of head-
lamps / you throw on faith / defy your fate / then brake lights
flash / then red eyes burn / you raise your head / a tire iron
blurs / you're running / tumbling / slicing through weeds / the
silhouette behind you / a half-

step / behind / an owl / a raven / a bruja / a demon / as your
grandmother warned / if you summon darkness / it will turn
its head / you pray to the portrait in the hallway box / wristwatch / ashtray / thin tarnished sword / a crack in a fence /
opens wide as a door / you roll inside to the opposite side / the
streetlamp pulses / an altar of shadow / kneeling on the curb /
you offer your own. /

*

/ Becoming scared all over again / slipping back home /
through a hole in the screen / your mother asleep / beneath

painted-glass windows / her silent Mary watches you pass /
while the dimes from your pockets / spill stars on the floor /
the toads in the ditch / finish singing their song / the casual-
ties of crawling / toward moths / toward light / dreaming like
seeds / embedded in clay. /

Imprint

1. Walking like weeds along Guadalupe Trail with jackets of bark and jackets of leaves their hat brims as sharp as the edge of the mesa with sand in their mouths where once there was water you watch them through the dust on your screen. Solitary men beneath a burnt orange sky dragging cottonwood shadows still following home the bead on the bottle of a longneck Coors from a bowling alley bar where the maps of their lives like the scars on their fingers from pushing too deep in their pockets for change. You think they can't see you but somehow they do and that's what scares you the tilt of their heads the crease in their eyes the absence you feel as they wait for your face to emerge.

2. You remember the first one you saw on the ditch bank maybe four or five on the backyard swings with two of your sisters singing "Can't Buy Me Love" and "I Want to Hold Your Hand" while your mother's shoulders glisten with oil. She is tending her roses in the first fragile days after your father dies all the windows just opening to spring. From the cobweb-cottonwoods behind your back fence he adds his voice

to your own with a face of black ash raising fists of crinkled brown paper. Your mother gathers you up and herds you inside while the dial spins on her phone. His spider eyes wink as you peek through the screen and he smiles as if he knows you.

3. Your grandmother warns you while you play near the screen be careful of what you allow into your life. Because darkness is real just like there is light and you never know what can creep in. And she never even laughs when she talks of El Cocoman wandering the fringes for life. After she says it you aren't sure what to believe until she slips out her silver cross and kisses it.

4. All the men in your family lost fathers too young and spent their lives following the pull of a calling driving too hard to drown out the sound. You don't know if you hear it but sometimes you think you do in the dust on your screen as it rises.

5. He steps from the dusk with buttons like tears and cracks open his knothole mouth. Words of wet moths dribble onto the ditch bank burrowing deep as if they had fingers. You back into the diamonds of your chain-link fence on your way late coming from school. He extends his palm like the dried tongue of the llano and unscrews an eye made of stone. He is telling you something or offering you something from the nest of leaves wreathing his chest. But the absence inside you keeps spiraling down as you scramble to make the right side. He never sees the nails you buried with your mother to keep a safe space for the swings. When he steps forward toward you the spike through his sole sends tremors splitting open his

seams. You never ask what he asks or see what he holds and his scar glistens inside you like rain.

6. If you knew how to pray you would offer one here for the purgatory souls still following your trail after one thousand miles and one thousand dreams like the smoke from cedar incense you light like a candle to purify a past when you raised your hand in a gesture hello or maybe goodbye to the solitary men in your ink-wash portraits dribbling from the edge of your page.

7. The last time you visit Guadalupe Trail you stand as a father looking down into the ditch at the windblown nest of plastic wrappers and broken bottles trying too hard to smile. And just over your shoulder through the drainpipe tunnel a neon shimmer in a pothole puddle where something like a sigh starts trying to tell you to rake your fingers through the ashes and bone. So you kneel in the clay and touch something like warmth which feels like enough with both palms pressing so you leave your imprint with their own. Rising at last you glance back at your old screen in your driftwood and denim and part the weeds for your own journey home.

IV

ALTAR OF LEAVES

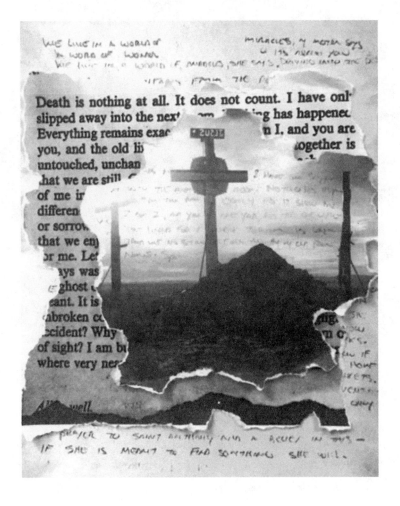

The Crossing

1.

I keep my
hands like this so
they won't fly
away from the llano to the
blue-eyed ocean
but I won't let them until they can
fold the regrets I carry into
the fist of a rose.

2.

The salt cedar brush
looks a lot like fire,
wreathing the open heart
of the valley
pulsing white-gold,
like a kitchen-wall Jesus,

two fingers testing the wind,
but I still have faith
in the brown necklace river,
and the path it cuts
through the plains
feeling along the
collarbone mesa,
for the scar left behind
from the chain.

3.

The sand around here
is so sad and white,
windblown faces
of dough and holes,
all staring up from
stiff-backed pews,
all wondering
what I might do.

4.

I saw a day moon rising
above the Manzanos,
like a thumbnail

on my outstretched hand,
from the time I jumped
from the arroyo's edge,
not caring
if I would land.

5.

When I was born, Papá
prayed for a son, and raised me with
knuckles and denim, but what I
really wanted was to leave like a man, without
ever turning my head.

6.

I know it's hard for you
to stand there like that
with your back so close to the
river, but like I said
in the truck, it's not the current
you watch,
but the stillness
pulling you under, then there's how
it swallows sheep and goats
whole, but try not to

worry, I know how to part
the shimmering
seams of the fold.

7.

The crease in this photo
could be a barbed wire scar,
or a crossroads
crossing my life,
but I was just folded
into somebody's pocket,
and held there
close as a knife.

8.

A moment ago
on our way to fiestas,
the flatbed got stuck
off the trail,
my stubborn brother
cutting corners again,
but that doesn't mean
we're destined to stay,
I'll weave a blanket

from the Bethlehem stars,
and in my bare feet
lead us away.

9.

I used to believe
after I died
I'd find gold among
the camposanto stones,
buried in jars
with seeds of light,
nestled in thickets of bone,
but now before bed,
there's my nightstand teeth,
and the gallstones I saved
from the doctor,
and sorrowful Mary
trying to smile,
while I lower my head
and go under.

10.

Tomorrow, I will
pack the dress and the shoes,

and tie my hair tight in a bun,
then milk the cows, feed the chickens,
gather feathers from the dust,
breathing through sweat and flies,
and with both hands
open to the oil drum smoke,
offer my name, Desolina,
to the sky.

Slightest Edge

1.

If you unfolded the creases I have carefully pressed, apricots
would spill from the spouts, with concrete dust, brown river
clay, and the Navajo ring of the sky, all sewn together with
barbed wire thread to hold me tight at the seams, through cur-
rents of smoke, asphalt, and oil

    coins in a mountain stream.

2.

You know, that door behind me, it never quite closes, it's like
a dog following you home from the pueblo, friendly enough,
sniffing your hands, flashing teeth at the scent of regret, but I
don't really mind it, the shadow at my back, and how it pushes
and pulls like the wind, we have long conversations through
sand, scrub, and cholla

    shouldering all I have been.

3.

I was thinking just now, of the sunrise apples, just outside the
Santa Fe boarding school walls, wreathed in feathers we could
never reach
  how they fell to the ground like bells.

4.

Let me tell you a story, about thirty years from now, when I
will visit my daughter's Albuquerque home, sitting back in her
rocker, with my longneck Coors, her pet owl will fly from the
closet, and holding out my finger, it will hop right on, staring
up as if we had met, when I ran away as a boy to the yellow
hills of Marquez, with my bedroll and apple all alone, asleep in
a cave beneath a mural of Our Lady,
  warmed by the bluest stones.

5.

A minute ago, wetting my hair in the mirror, I saw my family
sitting at supper, my two little sisters, my mother when young,
the man of smoke she married, all smiling, all milk and silver,
while I watched from fencepost mud, but beyond my reflection, of mothwing dust,
  a sky burning brighter than blood.

6.

The coffee around here tastes a lot like the smoke, from the
oil drums hobos burned in the fields, each of us grasping, at
feathered ashes,
>so white we could almost believe.

7.

After you died, I used to believe you'd slip into the crack of a
windshield, a silver shard revealing itself, at the perfect turn
of the wheel, but when you reached out, the shard slid away, a
painless slice in your finger, and yet I still believe, it's the shine
that endures,
>that the clouds on my shoes will linger.

8.

There's a spider in the corner, her hourglass turned, to start
this all over again, driving up north, through alfalfa and apples,
as the dirt road splits from its hem, then I rise from the wheel,
in a loving wind, warm as wax, in a puddle of sun,
>radiating out from within.

9.

I know it seems as though I am talking in riddles, but really
that's not how I am, it's just that being back in Corrales, after
so long away, feels like these cracks in the walls, there's the
scar of the grain, and what everyone sees, split open dark as
night, but within the gaps, tabletop candles,
    trembling fingers of light.

10.

Tomorrow I'll step down from these worn pine steps and
enter a river of stones, and faces will blur as they watch me
pass, erasing the boy left alone, Carlos the orphan will become
Charlie Boy the man, and no one will think him as strange,
inside his pockets, his skin will brush
    silver contours of change.

11.

One last thing, which makes me wonder, this photo appears to
be broken, a brick through the lens of an in-between life, but
it's more like a space has just opened, standing here now on
the slightest edge, it's all just ice on the window, sliding away
with memory's emulsion
    a sigh released from cinder.

Water for Roots

I.

My grandfather's smile is a thing made of silver beneath a sun-cured brim as wide as a mesa cooling buckskin skin slicked wet with an acequia flowing so deep he will not be emptied into fields of beans or the flatbed Ford delivering peaches and concrete his will is his weapon his square-shouldered pose itself an achievement or something like pride his young family beside him an embrace he long sought so hot so tired in Depression-era denim in the folds of these furrows he will build their first home from blocks of terrón laid tight as his fist trying too hard to hold a fourth daughter drowning in rheumatic fever dreams just one more ghost weighting his pockets no matter how many times he crosses the Mohave to feed nine mouths painting battleships gray his wife will still chase the chrome wheels rolling to the dimes-slot horizon of the Pacific Ocean seam but in this one moment he owns his own shine even decades into the future refusing to fade.

II

The weight in her arms I can feel the weight she adjusts her arms her bare branch arms she centers her hips to try to bear it my grandmother carved from bone from shadow glancing not forward nor sideways nor back but scanning the horizon for somewhere to rest for anywhere to rest a bird or a cloud or a bright budding bee her face molded hardened resigned exhausted the baby my mother her third of nine children her housedress cinched as tight as her smile this is not what she saw this is not what she dreamed when she stared out the window of her father's rancho at prairie hawks gliding so effortlessly forward so open so free she could finally breathe yet her bones still grow from cottonwood roots too stubborn to uproot and although she envisions the sapphire ocean she will eventually settle in this green bowl valley with a backyard garden of American Beauties and a statue of Mary whose robes hold the rain like pearls on a rose.

III

Can't overlook the children in the frame in their smart little suits in the white sailor hat in the white sailor skirt in Navy blue collar all dressed for a cruise in the New Mexican desert my little girl aunt and my little boy uncle and my infant mother with quizzical eyes all turned toward a lens none yet can read so none of them smile an odd juxtaposition to their rumpled parents which makes me wonder what they might

have been thinking in the summer of '36 as they stood with
their kids in the rancho fields the cute little kids all dressed
for a voyage like stepping off deck in San Pedro or Laguna
with palms and eucalyptus and orange grove breezes is this
what she thought as she buttoned their buttons as she saw
herself at the end of the pier my grandmother staring into a
sapphire summer of Pacific sun and what about my grandfather can he see the battleships as high as the Sandias in his
turpentine clothes painting dead-eye gray ships heading for
Iwo Jima and Guadalcanal carrying friends and brothers-in-
law to return like empty bottles wind whistling their souls but
no it's the children I want to talk about here the little children
called to attention pulled from their naps posed for a portrait
of exactly what perhaps the desires of their parents and friends
or props for an auntie heading back to the coast when all they
want is to continue their dreaming just look at them watching
the thought balloons rising to test the wind which way is it
blowing what happens next will they stay or go their frowning
expressions asking big questions nothing is set here everything
is possible Corrales or California let the compass needle spin
in this one little field each of them wondering what the emulsion might hold.

IV

I once made the mistake of calling this image a *Grapes of
Wrath* portrait of my mother and her family and she snatched
it back beneath the dining room lamp and said I was wrong

there were no grapes of nothing the Depression afflicted big cities or farmers near Oklahoma and Texas while her Rio Grande village had all it needed within the furrows and coops and pews and what I call poor was actually abundance and a self-sufficiency forgotten today and my own projection is my own rejection of faith and family and why am I pushing so hard into this frame what am I seeking a story or dream or a nostalgic distortion of what I have lost or never had but wait I told her that's not what I meant I was seeking resilience rising up from hard ground and harvested here with a shutter blade click while spiraling words chip through distance and time like water for roots like a stalk of dried grass or a milkweed laid bare on the surface to find its way toward the light toward the soil that blossoms in a moment suspended in gray meant for blue.

A Place She Goes

Only one of three images of my mother as a girl she dealt to me once on her dining room table like a hand of poker after finally visiting after ten years away to walk beside her on the ground we still walk the only ground we can walk the tratteggio of a time I cannot have and cannot hold but am allowed to copy with a portable scanner of white light swallowing this glimpse she allowed like the space in a mirror between silver and glass flashing open flashing wide at just the right angle for the briefest of moments my passage through to the other side.

*

It's the fingers that get me it's the fingers that wound the pale child fingers barely even there in the center of the frame I can almost feel the tickling daisies through the fading-erasing-dissolving white wing of overexposed emulsion from a sister or a brother or a long dead cousin reaching out to my mother to make her grin or make her laugh at something unsaid or something unseen a joke or a burp say cheese for the camera it's good to see her happy in a moment like this a piece of evidence of something like joy but also sad and a little unset-

tling the absent presence taking so much away nearly half of
this frame consumed by smoke from an oil drum fire of forgotten things or maybe the glare from the stained-glass row
of receding prayers and yes it is tempting to call it the loss I
know is coming on the hot llano wind to tremble the candles
of bedside lilies where her little sister wheezes rheumatic cotton breath and her aunt's high heel slips on the tracks of a
departing train and my much older father smiles through cigarette pneumonia and her Parkinson's parents sleep with crosses
on their pillows but that's not what I see it's more that her
portrait will find its own balance with negative space bringing
into focus all that she has and all she has lost by granting her
the most beautiful dreams and a way of seeing so clear in the
dark.

*

I know this expression I have seen many times so young in
this photo maybe six or seven on the broken stone steps of her
grandfather's rancho on the edge of the river soaking in the
sun the woodsmoke the apples she turns from the lens and
she's already drifting already dreaming already gone to a place
she goes a wagon wheel road in the Rio Puerco badlands as
deep as a mirage hugging barrels of peaches on a flatbed Ford
with sundial shadows and barbed wire wind her sanctuary
place she is making this memory as bright as the key to the
carved bone box she will one day discover in a porcelain jar by
the pendulum clock and the dripping rosaries to turn to me
beaming saying she thought it was lost.

Altar of Leaves

1.

Poised on the foothills the Sandia Mountains for all that awaits on the rim of her twenties the sun on her shoulder Rio Grande Valley below a barbed-wire stitching of alfalfa and chile yet her gaze remains fixed on the western horizon on a red-winged hawk or a plume of smoke or the faintest smudge on the white canvas sky a root spiraling down to the village she left but will seek her whole life in the tributary scars on her grandfather's fingers the cataract clouds in her grandmother's eyes the family saints with blood on their knees with both hands behind her she fiercely holds on.

2.

Hard not to make too much of the shadows rising behind from juniper and piñon to slip into her pockets prescient warnings of dead aunts and lost cousins who will knock on her screen and sit on her bed to talk about everything and nothing at all and all she can see but cannot possibly know the sensation she will have in late middle age when finding the brass key to the carved bone box holding purple velvet pouches of engagement rings constellations of silver she will slide on her fingers while the rain drips down from her trumpet vine window.

3.

I know how this ends which is why I return to wind and
rewind the moment before she crosses the crosswalk on the
downtown street from the library to the drugstore for sand-
wich and Coke where a man in a white smock with sad eyes
and Pall Malls reaches across the counter from his loss to hers
from his dead wife and brother and entire family line to her
sister and cousin and aunt on the tracks closing the distance of
twenty-five years between them while screen credits roll Cary
Grant and Grace Kelly *It Takes a Thief* if I could offer a prayer
it would be in the moment when the aperture holds the swell
of light and the pharmacy door opens to a bell.

4.

Six decades from this moment her sandal will catch on the jagged stone walkway beside her front door while watering her roses on a hot July day she will fall to both knees as if blinded by knives with two broken toes and a pair of gashes and two blackened eyes on the path she had laid to return to her village grown wild grown mean like one of her stray dogs but the worst of it is she will tell you over the telephone is finding herself in the green valley grass with the Sandia Mountains so impassively blue a reverse mirror image of this rose-colored frame of two strong women at opposite ends of a difficult life both of them gathering courage to rise.

5.

No, that's still not right maybe none of this is you may never enter this silent frame this ordinary frame this ordinary pose she is not interested in presenting herself in a way to be seen she reveals so little beyond an air of indifference or a confident composure some will call regal her way of surviving as a widow with five kids turning away from present to past to the infinite promise within the pause maybe that's it your final offering on this altar of leaves your relentless pursuit of how she endures it's the space your mother opens by averting her eyes.

V

CONFLUENCE

1

Awake again drawn back once
more to blue light seeping through
stained lace curtains and a black
spider dream on the dashboard
down from Denver to Albuquerque to visit your mother after a
decade away the damp sheet sweat
the smell of regret rolling over in
bed into the face of Mary a silent
candle a sorrowful burn you slip
on jeans for an apology gesture or
maybe forgiveness to irrigate her
yard of silver-leaf maple you walk
through her house of cedar smoke
apples and mothball cracks the
clock hands turn toward a barbed
wire crown and a wall of keys
while somewhere north a white
pickup rolls along the acequia if
you don't hurry you'll miss this
chance to bathe the roots binding
your ankles to ground you left but
never escaped.

[—a continuous flow—]

2

Watching yourself a boy of seven
stepping from sleep for the rit-
ual cleansing of river through
valley through corn squash and
beans your uncle rising with the
window sheet glow his crescent
wrench silver against head gate
bolt rust you follow him outside
goosebumps breaking dandelion
bright across bare arms bare legs
your pet ducks feel it too then
guinea hen peacock and flightless
geese charging the canal in morning star spray your toes planted
firm in firm brown soil wading
into the current so green.

                    [—*underlying feeling or*
                              influence—]

3

Staring from the edge your mother's acequia at a dog rib skeleton a
mud-splattered typewriter a balled
up sweater and seven bright bottles of Old Milwaukee the yellow grass reaching through the
nests of ghosts you saw as a boy
through your bedroom screen with
paper bag lips they whispered hello
like your father's things all packed
into boxes in the hallway closet his
ashtray wristwatch thin tarnished
sword all calling you back to wash
it clean with snowmelt from Jemez
so you jump in knee-deep into the
earthen canal to peel back layers
of guilt and nostalgia grown thick
with horse flies and crows while the
white pickup rolls just south of Bernalillo the sky apple green above the
Sandias bright as a cross a sign to
yourself there still might be time.

*[—medication to an
organ or wound—]*

. . . listen she says from a
memory shimmer driving deep
into the desert a badlands road
you and your mother feeling for
tracks from your grandfather's
boots through stone and cactus the
Dustbowl wind the devil's breath
his footfalls drag from boarding
school walls toward a pool of coins
a buckskin mesa his one oasis in a
life of sand you need his story his
pathway home your mother has
seen it she knows the way the hid-
den wellspring Los Ojitos she says
she will show you the way you
drink her words as if they were
water from hills of salt a seed
unfolds . . .

*. . . across your windshield a
sun-streaked reel a wisp of khaki
your grandfather turns his driftwood shoulders he opens his mouth
a bee unfolds on the edge of the
dashboard you turn to your mother
you see her unseeing instead reliv-
ing gemstones gathered with
grandchildren and nieces a different story a different time each
of you seeking a different end the
wind between you smiles with
teeth the serrated horizon saws on
the bones of the visions you hold so
close to your chest you almost hear
them breathing your name . . .*

4

You cannot contain it this run-on
haunting jumping the berms of the
columns you dig you might as well
spoon up her sighs with your fingers
nourishing yourself on sepia-stained
air and yet you still grip your uncle's
irrigation shovel to shepherd the flow
of her words in your sleep her words
in your sleep you no longer belong she
says in your sleep the roots you seek
have all been severed by the choices
you made and prayers you shunned yes
it is sad you now want to drink with
both hands the current running deep
through her life but the tap has been
turned the acequia run dry the hands
on her clock have rusted to nails.

*[—artificial ridge or
embankment—]*

. . . yet you see him so clearly
his khakis so clearly with both
hands drinking a pool of clouds
beyond the badlands a green bowl
valley a barbed wire veil the end
of his crossing the crack of a fen-
cepost a bee unfolds as he lowers
his head to pass . . . through . . .

5

On the acequia shoulder just over your
shoulder a dust devil hisses through beer
bottle teeth you gather up trash as the
brown earth ripples with broken nickels
like hypnotist coins just off to your left
a roadrunner lands with obsidian eyes
pooling centuries deep he is bringing
you something offering you something
inside its black beak a black spider runs
on the dashboard down to your childhood home where a water vessel falls
into one thousand screams on hands
and knees your mother recovers a labyrinth of shadows to seal the shards
of the medicine bird once balanced on
heads of Zuni women carrying the river
without spilling a drop she fills in the
cracks so no one will see the roadrunner
swallows the spider on the ditch bank
delivering its message of X tracks in the
dirt like a path through the thorns of
your mother's backyard blooming bright
as the blade of a votive candle flame.

*[—medicine bird's
X-shaped tracks con-
ceal its direction from
malignant wind—]*

[—despite evidence
beyond evidence—]

                              . . . *above the mesa of charred*
                              red rock two braids of smoke two
                              hawks in flight coming together
                              coming undone a snake between
                              them dangling between them you
                              and your mother dance in the
                              silence a cursive elusive both of you
                              knowing just how to read . . .
[—an experience of—]

. . . *we're here she says at a*
cattail pond of mud flies and weeds
Los Ojitos she says but when you
follow her outside your vision stag-
nant as the algae-stained surface
what's wrong she asks just look at the
sand with so many colors a ceremo-
nial maze or a Pollack painting she
gathers pebbles of salmon and sage
just take one she says a piece of this
ground a shard of Los Ojitos but all
you can see is the pyrite promise of
her story-illusion just take it she says
to remember . .

[—seeing—]

. . . *kneeling alone the pond*
eye rheumy the crack in your stone
the crack in her stories you want to
believe still trying to believe above
the mesa two hawks in flight
skimming the water splitting the
seam of all you perceive you dip
your hands and for a moment you
see it you almost breathe it the
shimmer between it tipping back
your head you begin to taste it
the salt on the rim of your grand-
father's canteen . . .

. . . *at your boots near the pond a sun-*
rise snake a turquoise snake as smooth
as a ring unmoving or dead you stop
in your tracks seeking hawks overhead
your mother leans in close it's an omen
she says a gift she says for your new
home she says with both hands you
hold the sky made flesh . . .

[—an experience of—]

6

. . . listen your mother says on the highway home to the story you
seek after your father died she drove into the desert losing herself
to find herself at Jemez Pueblo before an old man of cedar sitting
apart with a display of gourd rattles he had carved from his dreams
a menagerie of turtles and owls and roadrunners their expressions
so alive with black-and-white light how beautiful she said through
a mask of grief so he asked her to choose from among his blankets
her fingertips settled on a wing-feathered snake with silver-coin
eyes its tail as long as a sunrise river what is it she asked to his
half-moon smile you have chosen well the flying serpent between
both worlds bringer of water wind rebirth . . .

7

Standing at last on your mother's acequia the wind rasp fading the drainpipe draining the white pickup idling the ditch boss's shovel a sword in the sun you hold your breath as water arrives its foam flowers swallows beer bottle bones and alphabet teeth the current rising on a sigh of bees in your mother's yard the liquid adobe a carpet of diamonds on soil of thorns too rusted to drink she watches you behind her stained lace curtains her gaze as heavy as her past on your shoulder so you kneel head low and offer her this an experience of seeing a gesture of believing with two fingers rubbing a coin from the river a bead of silver into this ground a seed of your heart.

VI

EXCAVATION

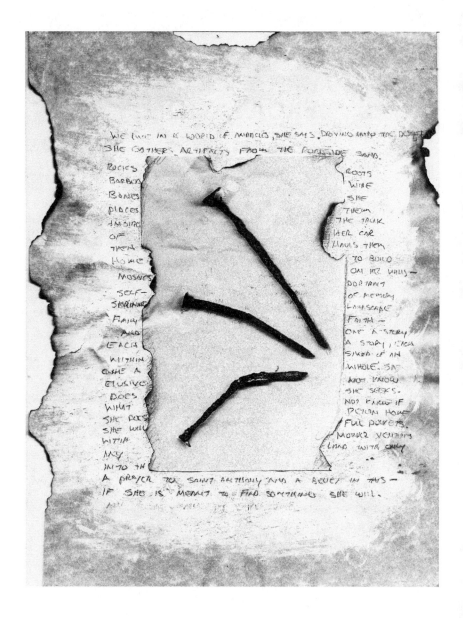

Near the village of Amalia at a roadside chapel hollowed by fire you stand with your daughter in a bell tower grave the roofless sky impassively blue the adobe walls glazed black with soot beneath your boots a garden of nails a garden of clippings from your grandmother's roses she watched you turn from her nightstand Mary her candles trembling with doubt and regret you kneel in thorns to gather a bouquet to hand to your daughter asking what does she see and she tells you she sees the wings of a moth the curve of the moon the marble saints bearing silent witness to woodstove embers a blossom of bees the ash-choked chimney releasing its sighs very good you say as your mother once said when you pulled from home soil a rust-stained root she turned to tell you it's not what you look at but what you see in the iron spike on your palm a clock hand ticks across the crease a compass needle moving steadily back to the place you stand the sanctuary walls all burned to the ground leaving only the memory of the weight once held.

Leaving only the memory of the weight once held you held you pull from white dunes overlooking the river a root of chamisal stripped black brushed clean by blue smoke and ash its skin midnight silver in noonday sun a double exposure what resided below now raised to the surface its own resurrection of all who looked down where your mother was born vaqueros farmers and Anasazi hands all drink from the bowl of sky river mountains the tempestuous llano where you once stood as a boy your fingers deep in sand spiraling down trying to feel for the current a testament of will and stubborn denial both of you shaped by the path of your reaching.

Both of you shaped by the path of your reaching you
and your mother on the Galisteo plains bullet holes hissing
through No Trespassing signs you plant your boots on barbed
wire fence opening a space to lower yourselves through the
veil of memory or story or dream the dirt shimmers silver
where her grandfather once walked toward a wall of stones on
the yellow horizon a hacienda outpost against Navajo raids the
blood runs deep through the insatiable sand she turns to tell
you if only you could see between white lines of history you
too could reclaim this past she seeks she bends to one knee
to dip her palms in a puddle of rust removing a loop of Spanish cursive a flourish of thorns woven in steel she wants you
to translate you tell her a noose or a graveyard or a warning
for disturbing this place this sacred space she begins to laugh
the ghosts in these ruins are not that malicious they once were
her people what you have is the latch to a back door fence or
a hidden gate or a secret passage or a shortcut home consider
yourself lucky what you hold in your hands is actually a key.

What you hold in your hand is actually a key drawn first by color and then by weight to an oval of ochre in the hot Marquez sand a vein of rust a branch of blood centering its halves like the arroyo you crossed with both sides connected by the thinnest root still intact still surviving near the mural of Mary on blue-painted walls with her hands pressed tight against peeling prayers the sanctuary cave where your grand-father slept after crossing the desert from orphanage stalls you can almost feel his pulse in your fingers through the pollen grains worked deep into your skin.

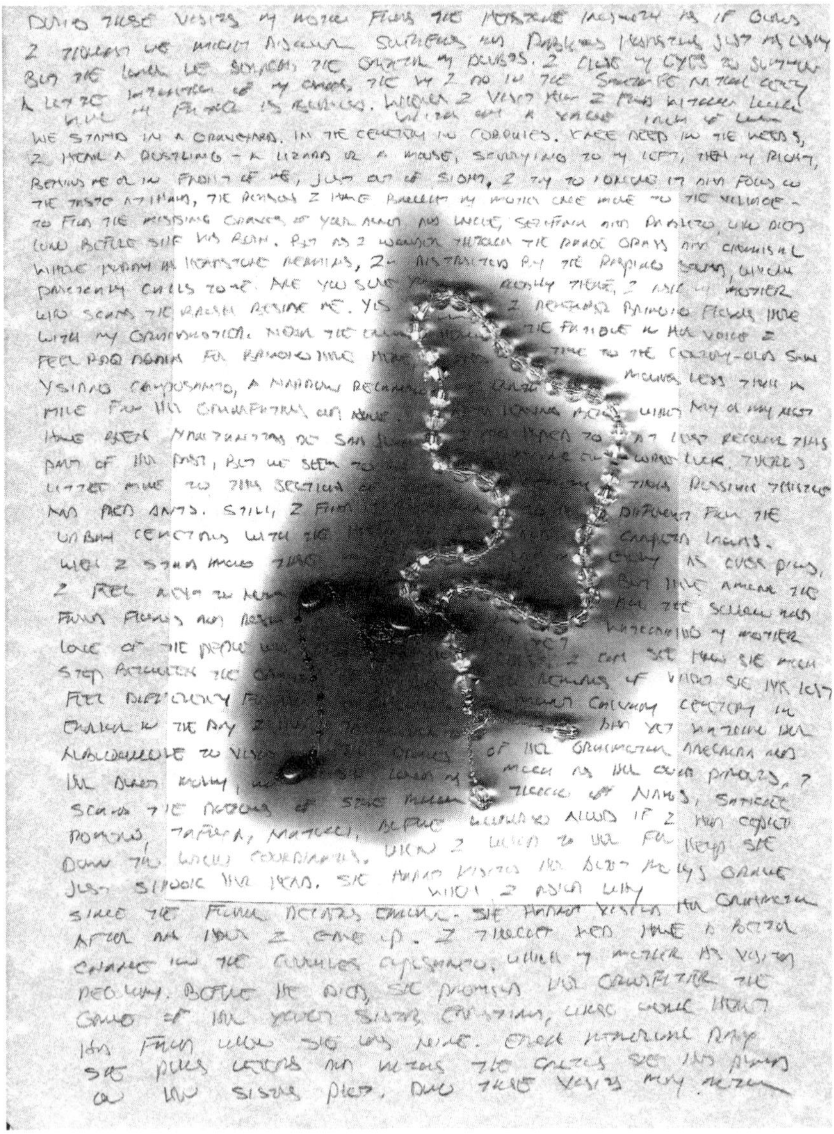

A pollen of grains worked deep into your skin the river at Los Ranchos the stained-glass sky the hymn of the llano between your fingers a liquid chain an absent cross misplaced or lost or never actually worn its burden enough to keep you following the faint reflection of all you lost.

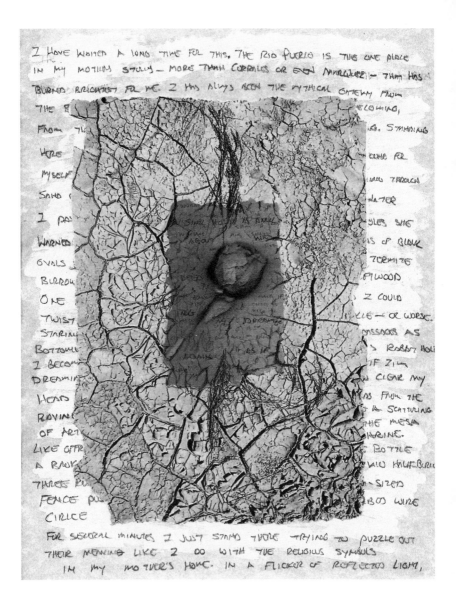

I HAVE WAITED A LONG TIME FOR THIS. THE RIO PUERCO IS THE ONE PLACE
IN MY MOTHER'S STORY — MORE THAN CORRALES OR EVEN ALBUQUERQUE — THAT HAS
BURNED BRIGHTEST FOR ME. I HAS ALWAYS BEEN THE MYTHICAL GATEWAY FROM
THE E...   ...GLOWING,
FROM TH...   ...S. STANDING
HERE   ...COME FOR
MYSELF   ...WAY THROUGH
SAND   WATER
I PAS...   ...OLES SHE
WARNED   ...S OF BLOOD
OVALS   TERMITE
BURROW   ...FIWOOD
ONE   I COULD
TWIST   ...LE — OR WORSE.
STARING   ...MASSACRE AS
BOTTOM...   ...A RABBIT HOLE
I BECOM...   ...IF ZI...
DREAMING   ...CLEAR MY
HEAD   ...AS FROM THE
ROVING   ...A SCATTLING
OF ART...   THE MESA
LIKE OFFER...   SHRINE.
A BACK...   BOTTLE
THREE...   ...AND HALF BURIED
FENCE PO...   ...SIZED
CIRCLE   ...BOS WIRE

FOR SEVERAL MINUTES I JUST STAND THERE TRYING TO PUZZLE OUT
THEIR MEANING LIKE I DO WITH THE RELIGIOUS SYMBOLS
IN MY MOTHER'S HOME. IN A FLICKER OF REFLECTED LIGHT,

The faint reflection of all you lost your mother's first memory a chipped white cup a thicket of thorns the thin ruffled blossoms unevenly matched irregularly shaped the fragrance of mass she empties her water onto insatiable sand the sorrowful mysteries pour from her fingers her grandmother and sister and eventually her husband outside her window one rose for each child the wild one angry one joyous one silent one the faintest shimmer of nurturing bees she offers a cutting to press between pages cupping your hands to enfold its flame.

Cupping your hands to enfold its flame a shard of white earth from the toe of your boot at the acequia's curve a labyrinthine stripe once part of a vessel now shaped by the break its black-and-white edges your coordinates home against your palm you align the lines the tributary topography of the Rio Grande Valley grafting its contours assembling the whole.

VII

INHERITANCE

1.

I have a name
Once sent with a letter
From a Route 66 flat
Where a man sits alone
On a davenport couch
With Pall Mall upholstery
Trouser leg crossed
While he waits for the ember
To redden his skin.

2.

I have a name
Passed down on a ladder
Of men handing buckets
Of cigarette smoke
To sons left standing
In thresholds of flame
They could extinguish
Themselves
By walking away.

ghosted with dust gazing out into the morning sky. I held my breath not wanting it to break the offerings I so carefully arranged. Sliding to the side to make a small space, I blinked and the bird was gone, no heirloom disturbed, no evidence at all, just a breeze, and a clear glass spot of sun

I painted my father's face as the centerpiece of a resting place shrine, as hope and the one memory I had worn thin from decades of rubbing. I arranged my brushes like the heirlooms he left - brass keys, silver ashtray and *cracked turquoise ring* - but once I began, I could not face the face that was so much like my own – the smile like my smile, the cleft in my chin, and the dark eyes gazing out of the frame, beyond the horizon, just over my shoulder, at answers I never finding.

She grieved through music, through strong winds and storms, full volume through cloth console speakers. It was startling to see, the crescendo of passions, while my mother hand-waxed our hardwood floor. The planks had been laid by my father himself, imported from a mill in Iowa. By the time he left that home to find another, **twenty years before he met my young mother. Dr. Zhivago was her soundtrack of choice, the song of a love not meant to live.**

A bird visited my father before my mother, with feathers and **sapphire** eyes. It waited outside his diner drugstore and my young mother arrived. When he turned his brass keys it followed him inside to the soda fountain counter in back. It hopped on a stool while his Pal Mal smoldered and fed it potato chips by hand. Customers marveled at the serene little bird, "So tame as if it already knows you."

I unlocked the studio to my descanso shrine and stopped dead in the door. On the portrait with keys, ashtray and ring, a bird of white and silver. It opened its beak, half spread its wings, and locked its dark wet eyes with mine. I looked around

for how it had entered, but found the all latches latched. It stood before a window ghosted with dust gazing out into the blue morning sky. I held my breath not

3.

I have a name
That never quite fit
Too snug on the chest
Too loose on the arms
Though it set me apart
In desks at school
From Esquivel and Garcia
Duran and Gallegos
Distinctive and sure
At the top of the page
A plaque on a mantel
A uniform badge
Pinned in place
Tight as a mask

4.

I have a name
Saying something of me
I cannot say of myself
Half roots unknown
Half history unseen
Half of a hole
Absence above
Below and
Between.

5.

I have a name
Biting hard with straight teeth
Immaculate rows
Immaculate markers
Where my father lies buried
Beneath tobacco-stained marble
Glistening like ice
In the dead of summer.

6.

I have a name
Like a white picket fence
Around an Iowa cottage
With a Missouri porch
A Scotch-moss lawn
A French-lilac garden
And an ill-fitting gate
Refusing to close
So when you slam it too hard
Everyone turns
As you look behind you
For someone to blame.

7.

I have a name
From a Union soldier
With Confederate leanings
A Masonic sword
Squinting like history
From an obituary frame
Eyes as sharp
As his lumber mill saw
Staining the horizon
With smoke from its blade.

8.

I have a name
Worn by an uncle
Who wrote red notes
In bible margins
Whispered through lips
Thick as wet worms
Blue lodge rites
Compass and cross
Its pages dust
I cannot breathe.

9.

I have a name
Passed from a father
Erased from his home
To heal a son
Who could not forget
The silver wristwatch
The silver sword
The silver ashtray
Stained with black ash
So thick in his fingers
It might have been soil.

10.

I have a name
That knew I'd come looking
In the roadside weeds
Of the Arkansas town
Where my father was born
Clear-cut gnawing
The bone of neglect
Skull-socket windows
Backwash wind
A $100 bill
Calling me down
To acknowledge its face.

11.

I have a name
Trying hard to speak truth
To the man with the pen
Refusing to see
That the man on the page
Is exactly who
He appears to be.

VIII

BORDERLAND

SHE DROVE INTO THE DESERT AFTER MY FATHER DIED, HOUR AFTER HOUR
ALONG THE ASPHALT ARTERIES OF NORTHERN NEW MEXICO. SHE TOOK NO MAP
——————————— RELIED INSTEAD, AS SHE ALWAYS HAD ON MEMORY

HER FINGERS SPREAD AT HER SIDES, HER HANDPALMS DUG INTO
THE COARSE BLONDE SAND. I STOOD BESIDE HER THEN,
WATCHING THE WORRY LINES FADE FROM HER FACE AND
WITH MY ARMS WIDE I WAITED FOR THE CURRENT.

ROOTS

Smoke-thin memories penciled fast as you can while your mother breathes ghosts from the end of the phone line you feel but can't touch the words on the paper burrowing like seeds for who you are and who she was and why you left your left ear goes numb to the sudden silence the celestial static the distance between you laid bare on the page.

HEIRLOOM

Lock half-buried in the Galisteo plains where Navajos fought Spanish and Anglos who also fought Spanish and Anglos you straddle the line of history's frontline you and your mother trace her grandfather's tracks through snake weed and yucca toward a ruin of stone with yellow-stained wind through No Trespassing teeth you dip both hands in a puddle of rust to see your reflection ripple generations deep but a keyhole drains red sand through its eye a vision of a doorway long ago closed.

LANGUAGE

Mishmash of words all running together on hands and knees tumbling down the acequia on the way home from school Chicano boys chasing Anglo boys chasing coyote in the cross-hairs if only he could say it his own kind of truth an attempt at redemption an indirect direction a feinting a circling a doubling back to use the confusion to remain unseen while facing one way he heads in another lost in translation while no one is looking he slips beneath the bridge of his hyphen.

SANTOS

In frames on shelves on tabletop shrines hand-carved sorrow
hand-painted belief puddles of fire platters of eyes red dripping thorns on your mother's white walls always pulling you
back one bead at a time to the glow-in-the-dark rosary cupped
tight in your hands while green light fades where once burned
a faith the flame you felt was yours to hold.

ACCENTS

Rolled like dice hollowed of meaning but strategically weighted with just enough tildas to come up sevens as you scoop up the pot and get away clean before questions rise on razor blade wings and footfalls follow the holes in your story to the safe in your closet you left open a crack the combination spinning for everyone to read.

BRACELETS

Black labyrinth scoring on Zuni silver bands just pieces
of home you tell people who ask yet they might as well be
twin shackles of mirror the polished heat rising from asphalt
arroyos and acequia tracks across both wrists you trace with
your finger the language of edges from one town to another
one job to the next and still you feel the hammer the sawblade
flame melting many into one that's what matters that's what
you believe beneath the surface the shimmer is real.

ETYMOLOGY

Your wife gives voice to the word you seek the place you seek a Spanish hybrid of desire of want of sanctuary of strength of safety of soul where you know who you are and where you belong in the roots of your heart you share with your daughter the place you seek is *querencia.*

PERSONA

Return to the slur slurred over the phone by a man who read your newspaper column about chile and beans salted slightly with Spanish the way you were raised but your words didn't match your name in the paper your photo in the paper your skin in the paper so he called to inform you what New Mexicans call a mutt mongrel mix on the fringe of a village always stealing scraps always sneaking through spaces of other people's spaces a coyote he said a coyote he said that's all you are a coyote he said and the third time he said it stuck like the fur in the barbed wire fence in the teeth of the scar of your bloodline back so yes you finally said coyote is me.

IX

COYOTE

He emerges through a seam in the chain-link fence at the back of school after the library closes, the buses have left, and streetlights rub moths from their eyes. He looks to his right, then to his left, for the midnight blue Ford with the full-moon hubcaps prowling the cracks of the North Valley fault line, where Chicanos and Anglos smile with knives carrying resentment like chains in their fists. He can never find himself on one side or the other, with his thick auburn hair and porcelain skin and widowed brown mom who also looks white, and four siblings held together with patches. So he walks home alone along the edge of the acequia while the sun bleeds orange down the serrated edge of the mesa. He doesn't even hear it, the footfalls behind him, and by the time he turns around, there's copper on his tongue, bones in his teeth, and brake lights laughing at the curb. If only he can make it to the opposite bank they would never catch him in his sanctuary of weeds, but their grip is too tight, and the knee on his chest like a mountain. His only way out is the irrigation canal where none of them cross because the current is too strong mixing mud with sky with river. Yet the passage seems right, its own kind of becoming, so he launches himself as if he had wings while his skin sheds away with his jacket. Suddenly he can breathe suddenly he can sing held weightless mid-air in-between.

Epilogue

*One December evening, my mother brought home a dead cedar tree.
She cleared away the antique tables and chairs, shooed away our
stray dogs and cats, and anchored the trunk in the center of our living room in a washtub of rocks from the Rio Grande. And there it
stood throughout the holidays, as bent-backed and broken as a pil-
grim on the road to Santuario de Chimayo. She offered no explana-
tion beyond something about sculpture, and how Douglas firs had
become "too literal."*

*When I asked her about it, she placed a hand on my shoulder,
and encouraged me to see beyond what stood before me and instead
toward what it could become. I tried but couldn't get past the black
widow's eggs in the bark, or the way the torso leaned like one of
the men drinking whiskey behind our house on the ditch bank. Yet,
there were mornings she sprinkled piñon sawdust on the floor furnace, and in the gauzy haze of wood-smoke, the cedar tree became
a cross on the edge of the mesa marking ground where a spirit left
a body in a lightning storm and families visited with rosaries and
plastic flowers to help the soul find its way. In those moments, the
trunk resembled less a carcass than root, or a chrysalis.*

When it came time to decorate its branches, we set aside the plastic bulbs and electric lights from Kmart and crafted instead dozens of Ojos de Dios—small wooden "t's" woven together with cotton yarn into bands of turquoise and sunflower with vibrant centers of apple red and alfalfa green. The tradition came from the Huichol and Tepehuán people of Mexico, my mother said, and symbolized the eyes of God watching over the birth of a child—or the arrival of something new. Listening to her talk, I hung my ojitos as carefully as if I were lighting candles on an altar.

On Christmas morning, my mother poured a pitcher of warm water into the washtub, and the room filled with the scent of rain and soil from the llano, and in the white light of our broad front window, from stone, wood and cloth, a blooming.

MACHETE
Joy Castro, Series Editor

This series showcases fresh stories, innovative forms, and books that break new aesthetic ground in nonfiction—memoir, personal and lyric essay, literary journalism, cultural meditations, short shorts, hybrid essays, graphic pieces, and more—from authors whose writing has historically been marginalized, ignored, and passed over. The series is explicitly interested in not only ethnic and racial diversity, but also gender and sexual diversity, neurodiversity, physical diversity, religious diversity, cultural diversity, and diversity in all of its manifestations. The machete enables path-clearing; it hacks new trails and carves out new directions. The Machete series celebrates and shepherds unique new voices into publication, providing a platform for writers whose work intervenes in dangerous ways.

Finding Querencia: Essays from In-Between
HARRISON CANDELARIA FLETCHER

Eating Lightbulbs and Other Essays
STEVE FELLNER

The Guild of the Infant Saviour: An Adopted Child's Memory Book
MEGAN CULHANE GALBRAITH

Like Love
MICHELE MORANO

Quite Mad: An American Pharma Memoir
SARAH FAWN MONTGOMERY

Apocalypse, Darling
BARRIE JEAN BORICH